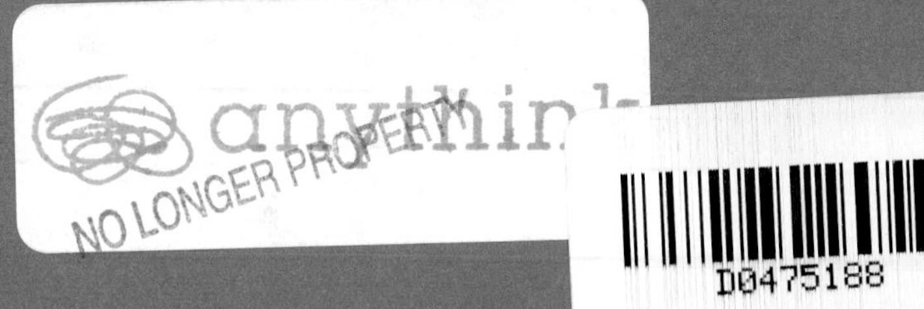
NO LONGER PROPERTY
D0475188

Writing Stories

Animal Stories

Anita Ganeri

Chicago, Illinois

an imprint of Capstone Global Library, LLC
Chicago, Illinois

Edited by Dan Nunn, Rebecca Rissman, and Sian Smith
Designed by Joanna Hinton-Malivoire
Original illustrations © Capstone Global Library 2013
Picture research by Ruth Blair
Production by Sophia Argyris
Originated by Capstone Global Library Ltd
Printed and bound in China by South China Printing Company Ltd

17 16 15 14 13
10 9 8 7 6 5 4 3 2 1

Library of Congress Cataloging-in-Publication Data
Ganeri, Anita, 1955-
Animal stories / Anita Ganeri.
pages cm.—(Writing stories)
Includes bibliographical references and index.
ISBN 978-1-4329-7530-2 (hardback)
ISBN 978-1-4329-7537-1 (paperback)
1. Animals—Fiction—Authorship—Handbooks, manuals, etc. 2. Children's stories—Authorship—Handbooks, manuals, etc. 3. Creative writing. I. Title.

PN3377.G36 2013
808.3—dc23 2012043110

Acknowledgments
We would like to thank the following for permission to reproduce photographs: Alamy pp.5, 7; Getty Images p.16 (Gary S Chapman); Shutterstock background images and design features, pp.4 (© Darrin Henry), 6 (© Abramova Kseniya), 8 (© Mat Hayward), 9 (© Zurijeta), 12 (© Eric Isselée), 14 (© Daniel Krylov), 16 (© Eric Isselée), 18 (© K Chelette), 22 (© Yuri Arcurs), 24 (© Sue McDonald), 26 (© Eric Isselée).

Cover photograph reproduced with permission of Shutterstock (© Eric Isselée).

Some words are shown in bold, **like this**. You can find out what they mean by looking in the glossary.

Contents

Follow this symbol  to read an animal story.

What Is a Story?

A story is a piece of **fiction** writing. It tells the reader about made-up people, places, and events. Anyone can make up a story. You need to choose a **setting**, some **characters**, and a **plot**. Then you can start writing.

There are many different types of stories. You can write mystery stories, funny stories, fairy tales, scary stories, adventure stories, and so on. This book is about writing animal stories.

Animal Stories

An animal story can be about a pet animal or about an animal that lives in the wild. You can base the story on your own pet, an animal that you have read about, or just your imagination!

Black Beauty is a famous book about a horse.

The Tortoise and the Hare is one of a collection of stories called Aesop's **Fables**.

Some stories use animal **characters** to teach a lesson. In *The Tortoise and the Hare,* a hare makes fun of a tortoise for being slow. The tortoise challenges the hare to a race. Thinking that he will win easily, the hare takes a nap, and then the tortoise wins the race.

Getting Ideas

Ideas for stories can come from books, the Internet, TV, or your imagination. Sometimes an interesting animal fact can spark a great story idea. Then you can do more research about the animals you are writing about.

Have you ever had a really good idea, then forgotten it? Keep a notebook and pencil handy for jotting down ideas. Then you will remember them when you are ready to write your story.

Plot Planning

What happens in your story is called the **plot**. It needs a beginning, a middle, and an end. Before you start writing, plan out your plot. You can use a **story mountain**, like the one below, to help you.

Middle
The main action happens. There may be a problem for one of your characters.

Beginning
Set the scene and introduce your main **characters**.

Ending
The problem is solved and the story ends.

Your story starts at one side of the mountain, goes up to the top, then goes down the other side.

A **timeline** is another way to figure out your plot. It can help you put the events in the right order. Here is a timeline for the animal story in this book.

A boy finds a stray dog on his doorstep.

↓

The boy hides the dog in his bedroom.

↓

Mom hears the dog barking.

↓

The dog chews Dad's best shoes.

↓

Dad says the dog has to go.

↓

The dog wakes the boy up at night.

↓

The dog warns the family about a flooded kitchen.

↓

Dad says the dog can stay.

In the Beginning

Your story needs a strong beginning. It should grab your readers' attention and make them want to keep reading. It is also where you introduce your main **characters**.

Can you turn any of these ideas into the beginning of a story?

Animal story ideas

- A stray dog appears on a doorstep.
- A girl gets an elephant as a pet.
- A tiger escapes from a zoo.

An Animal Story

There it was again. It sounded like a whimper, and it was coming from outside the front door. Joe went to the door and opened it. There, on the doormat, sat the scruffiest dog Joe had ever seen.

Keep the beginning of your story short so that it grabs your readers' attention right away.

Setting the Scene

The **setting** means the time and place where your story happens. It is like a world that you make up for your story. Writing about what your setting looks, sounds, and even smells like can help you bring that place to life.

An animal story might happen in a wild place, a zoo or wildlife park, or closer to home.

Joe looked up and down the empty street. Where was the dog's owner? Apart from a few cars, there was no one else around. It was getting dark. Street lights were flickering on.

Joe could smell rain in the air and heard a rumble of thunder. He couldn't leave the small dog outside in the cold and rain.

Imagining that you are in the setting can help you describe it.

Character Building

The **characters** in your story need to be interesting and believable. This is the same for human and animal characters. Think about what they look like, how they behave, and their likes and dislikes. Jot down the details in character fact files.

Character fact file
Character: Joe, a boy
Age: About 8 or 9
Looks like: Short, dark hair; wears glasses
Personality: Kind; funny; shy
Likes: Animals; soccer; watching cartoons
Dislikes: Bananas; homework

Character fact file
Character: Dog [no name]
Age: Unknown
Looks like: Small; brown fur; scruffy
Personality: Gentle; mischievous
Likes: Food; bones; being stroked
Dislikes: Having no home

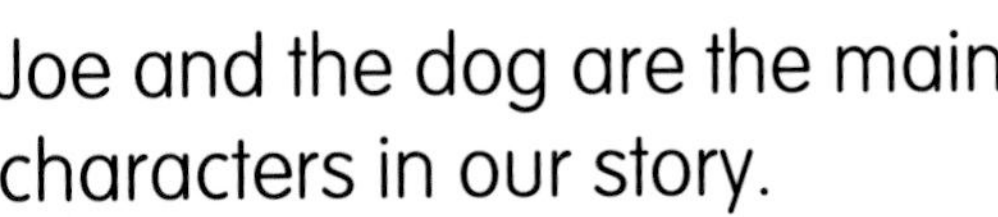
Joe and the dog are the main characters in our story.

The dog looked at Joe. It had scruffy, brown fur and a long tail that wagged and wagged.

It had big, sad, brown eyes. Joe had never had a pet before. He spent a lot of time on his own because he was shy and found it hard to make friends. But Joe loved the sad, scruffy dog as soon as he saw it.

Can you think of a name for the dog that describes what it looks like?

In the Middle

In the middle of your story, your **characters** face a problem. Here are some of the things that could go wrong in your animal story. Can you think of any other ideas?

Ideas for the middle of the story

Dog gets lost or is missing.

Dog behaves badly at home.

Dog's real owner turns up.

Dog gets injured.

Dog has to go to the vet.

One problem could be followed by another in your story.

Joe hid the dog in his bedroom. He called her "Scruffy." But Mom heard Scruffy barking. Luckily, Mom loved Scruffy, too.

"We can't keep her forever," Mom said. "But she can stay until we find her a new home."

Joe hoped that Mom would change her mind.

The middle of your story is also where the main action happens.

What Happens Next?

You might have several ideas for where your story will go next. How do you decide which is best? A **story map**, like the one below, can make it easier to work your ideas through.

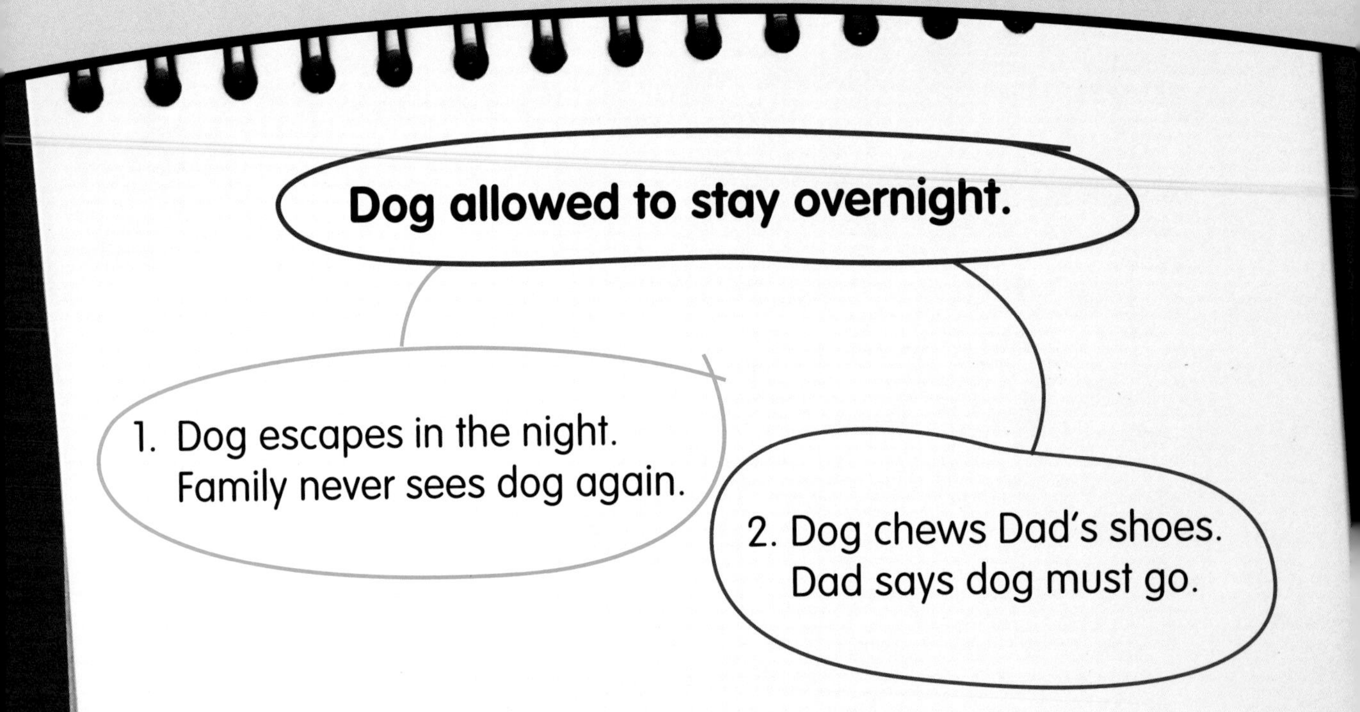

Dog allowed to stay overnight.

1. Dog escapes in the night. Family never sees dog again.

2. Dog chews Dad's shoes. Dad says dog must go.

You need to decide which direction your story will go in.

The next day, Joe rushed back from school to play with Scruffy. He threw a ball that Scruffy chased. Then Scruffy chased Joe around the backyard. Scruffy was smart, and Joe taught her to jump through a hoop. But Dad was angry at Scruffy. Scruffy had chewed a large hole in his best shoes.

Use your story map to move the story forward.

Speaking Parts

Use **dialogue** in your story to bring your **characters** to life. Dialogue means the words that people say. It can help show your characters' personalities. It also breaks up large chunks of text.

"She'll have to go," Dad said. "I'll take her to the animal shelter tomorrow."

Put **quotation marks** around the spoken words.

"She'll have to go," Dad said. "I'll take her to the animal shelter tomorrow."

"But, Dad," said Joe. "She likes it here. We're her family."

"Sorry, Joe," said Dad. "I've made my mind up."

Sadly, Joe went up to his bedroom. Scruffy followed behind.

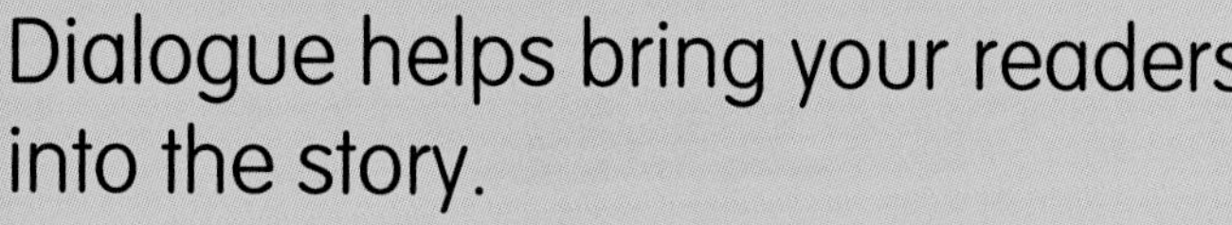

Dialogue helps bring your readers into the story.

Point of View

The story in this book is written in the **third person**. It is as if the writer is watching the action. Try retelling the story from a different point of view. You could pretend that you are Joe or Scruffy.

Joe's dad didn't want me to stay. I was very sad, and so was Joe.

These sentences are written from Scruffy's point of view.

In the night, Joe woke up suddenly. Scruffy was barking and scratching at the bedroom door.

"Ssshhh, Scruffy," said Joe. "You'll wake everyone up. And we're in enough trouble already."

But Scruffy kept barking. Joe opened the door and Scruffy ran into the kitchen. Joe saw water splashing. The faucet was on, and there was water all over the floor.

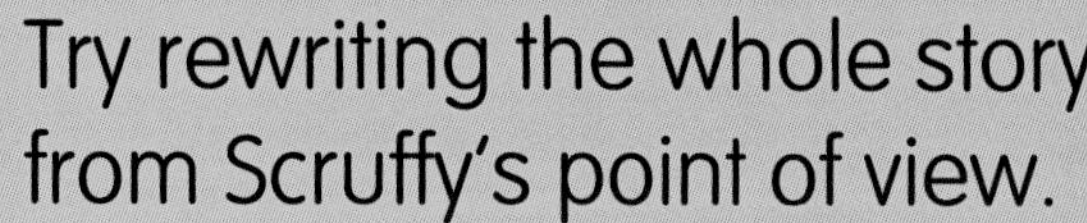

Try rewriting the whole story from Scruffy's point of view.

Happy Ending

The ending of your story is where you tie up any loose ends. It is also where your **characters** solve their problems. Your ending can be happy or sad, or have a clever or surprising twist. Here are some ideas for endings for the story in this book.

Endings

- Joe's parents still send Scruffy away.
- Scruffy becomes famous.
- Joe's parents get Joe a cat instead.
- Scruffy is allowed to stay.

Which ending would you choose?

Mom and Dad came running in. Everyone helped clean up the mess.

"I don't want Scruffy to go," said Joe, helping to mop the floor.

"Don't worry, Joe," said Dad. "Scruffy's a smart dog. If she hadn't woken us up, we would have had a flood. She can stay. And I'll get myself some tougher shoes!"

"Hooray!" cheered Joe. "Woof! Woof!" barked Scruffy.

Use your ending to tell your readers what happens to your characters.

More Top Tips

1 Writing strong animal **characters** is just as important as writing strong human characters. Having a picture of the animal can help you decide what it is like.

2 Read lots of animal stories by other authors. This will help to spark ideas and show you how other writers create good characters.

3 When you have finished writing, read and reread your story. Rewrite any parts that you are not happy with.

4 Use **adjectives** and **adverbs** to make your writing more exciting. You can also include a mixture of long and short sentences to keep your writing interesting.

5 If you get stuck, try some automatic writing. Write down whatever comes into your head and see what happens.

6 If you set your story in a real place, such as a rain forest, make your description as accurate as possible. This will bring the **setting** to life.

Glossary

adjective describing word that tells you about a noun (a noun is a naming word)

adverb describing word that tells you about a verb (a verb is a doing word)

character person in a piece of writing

dialogue words that characters say

fable story that has a message to teach

fiction piece of writing that is about made-up places, events, and characters

plot what happens in a story

quotation marks marks that show the words someone has spoken

setting time and place in which a story is set

story map diagram that helps you decide the next step of the plot

story mountain mountain-shaped diagram that helps you plan out a story

third person using "he," "she," or "they"

timeline list of events in the order in which they happen

Find Out More

Books

Ganeri, Anita. *Writing Stories*. Chicago: Raintree, 2013.

Stowell, Louie, and Jane Chisholm. *Write Your Own Story Book*. Tulsa, Okla.: EDC, 2011.

Warren, Celia. *How to Write Stories* (How to Write). Laguna Hills, Calif.: QEB, 2007.

Web sites

Facthound offers a safe, fun way to find Internet sites related to this book. All of the sites on Facthound have been researched by our staff.

Here's all you do:
Visit **www.facthound.com**
Type in this code: 9781432975302.

Index

By John Elway

with Greg Brown

Illustrations by Doug Keith

Taylor Publishing
Dallas, Texas

Greg Brown has been involved in sports for thirty years as an athlete and award-winning sportswriter. Brown started his Positively For Kids series after being unable to find sports books for his own children that taught life lessons. He is the co-author of *Dan Marino: First and Goal; Kerri Strug: Heart of Gold; Mo Vaughn: Follow Your Dreams; Steve Young: Forever Young; Bonnie Blair: A Winning Edge; Cal Ripken Jr.: Count Me In; Troy Aikman: Things Change; Kirby Puckett: Be the Best You Can Be;* and *Edgar Martinez: Patience Pays*. Brown regularly speaks at schools and can be reached at greg@PositivelyForKids.com. He lives in Bothell, Washington, with his wife, Stacy, and two children, Lauren and Benji.

Doug Keith provided the illustrations for the best-selling children's books *Things Change* with Troy Aikman, *Heart of Gold* with Kerri Strug, *Count Me In* with Cal Ripken Jr, *Forever Young* with Steve Young, and *Reach Higher* with Scottie Pippen. His illustrations have appeared in national magazines such as *Sports Illustrated for Kids*, greeting cards, and books. Keith can be reached at his internet address: atozdk@aol.com.

All photos courtesy of John Elway and his family unless otherwise noted.

Published by Taylor Publishing Company
1550 West Mockingbird Lane
Dallas, Texas 75235

Designed by Steve Willgren

A portion of this book's proceeds will go to the Elway Foundation

Library of Congress Cataloging-in-Publication Data

Elway, John, 1960–
Comeback kid / by John Elway with Greg Brown ; Doug Keith, illustrator.
p. cm.
Summary: The Denver Broncos quarterback, known for his come-from-behind victories, shares his triumphs and tribulations and offers advice on performing under pressure, winning and losing, and having a sense of humor.
ISBN 0-87833-983-3 (cloth)
1. Elway, John, 1960– —Juvenile literature. 2. Football players—United States—Biography—Juvenile literature. 3. Denver Broncos (Football team)—Juvenile literature. [1. Elway, John, 1960– . 2. Football players.] I. Brown, Greg. II. Keith, Doug, ill. III. Title.
GV939.E48A3 1997
796.352'092—dc21
[B]

97-27851
CIP
AC

Printed in the United States of America
10 9 8 7 6 5 4 3 2

Hi! My name is John Elway. Playing sports has taught me many lessons, including that ups and downs are to be expected.

During 14 seasons in the National Football League as quarterback for the Denver Broncos, I have won more regular-season games than any other starting quarterback in history. Still, three times I've felt the sting of losing a Super Bowl. Defenses fear my running, yet I have more yards going backward than forward.

This book is not meant to be my complete life story.

I've written this book to share with you the most important moments in my life, on and off the sports field, that molded me into the person I am today.

Football coaches often give inspiring halftime pep talks to their teams. Consider this book my pep talk to you.

Sunlit Ltd. © Ken Paul

Marc Serota/EGI

Winning the Super Bowl is the ultimate dream of all professional football players.

Three times I have played in Super Bowls with the Broncos and three times our team lost, all by lopsided margins, for a combined 136-40 score.

I understand in professional sports winning is everything. That comes with the paycheck. Until someone pays you to play, however, sports should not be only about winning.

After one of those crushing Super Bowl losses, a billboard in Denver, addressing our team, read: "How does it feel to embarrass a city?"

For me, when you give your all, losing is not embarrassing. There can be honor in defeat.

I think shame comes from failing to try, from giving up on yourself or those around you, from losing all hope.

Sports Illustrated, Jerry Watcher

Marc Serota/EGI

If you ask what's been my secret of success, most might say it's my God-given athletic ability to throw a football. While talent is important, it's not necessarily the most important thing. Thousands of talented people fail every day.

My strength has been my will to win—that competitive fire inside.

I never give up.

Going into the 1997 season, I've led 41 fourth-quarter comebacks, more than any other NFL quarterback before me. People call me the Comeback Kid for all those thrilling last-minute victories.

My hope is that after you read my story you will always remember that success in any field is just a comeback away.

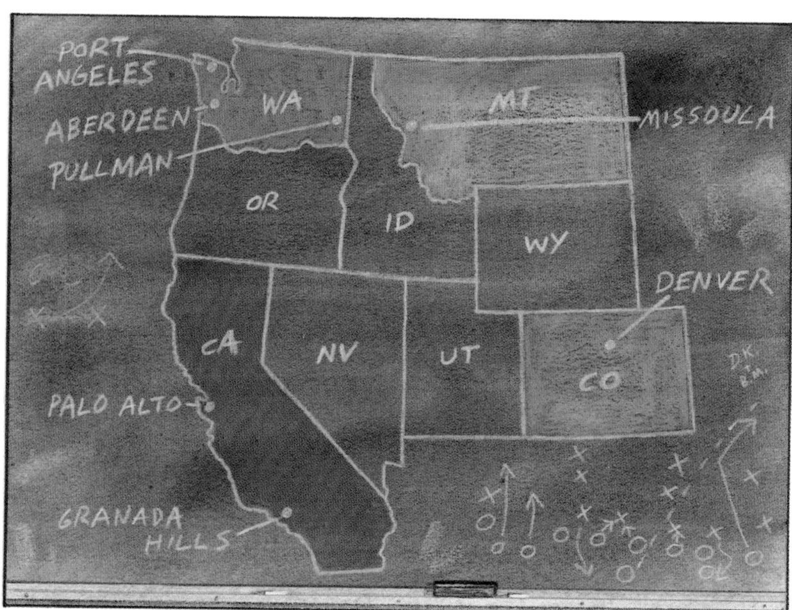

My story begins in the state of Washington. That's where my parents grew up, met, and married. My dad, Jack, was an outstanding high school and college quarterback. His father also played quarterback. My mom, Jan, played high school basketball and volleyball.

By the time I was born, on June 28, 1960, in Port Angeles, Washington, Dad had begun his career as a football coach, starting at the high school level. He later advanced to college coaching and eventually to the professional ranks, including joining the Broncos as a pro scout in 1993.

While Dad climbed the coaching ladder, we moved four times as I was growing up.

Washington State University, Athletic Media Relations

John's father, Jack, played quarterback at Washington State University before injuries cut short his career.

Identical vs. Fraternal

As you can see, Jana and I do not look the same. We are fraternal twins because we developed from two different eggs. Identical twins start as a single

I have two sisters. Lee Ann was the first born. Eighteen months later my twin, Jana, and I were born. I beat Jana into the world by 11 minutes, and we've been competing with each other ever since.

That's Jana and me pictured above at six months old. Can you tell which one is me?

Like everyone else, I crawled before I could walk. I did seem to enjoy our mini hot tub after a hard day on the carpet.

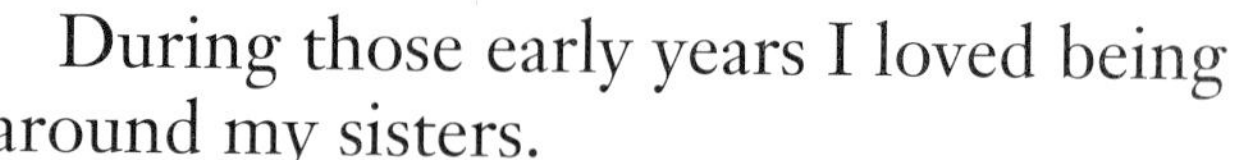

During those early years I loved being around my sisters.

This is the first house I remember—in Aberdeen, Washington. My sisters and I had great fun together. I'd do anything to play with them. I remember joining in on their tea parties. Hey, when you're the only guy you do what it takes to be included.

I didn't play with dolls, though. Not even G.I. Joes. Getting a toy truck one Christmas broke my heart. Anything that had a ball is what interested me.

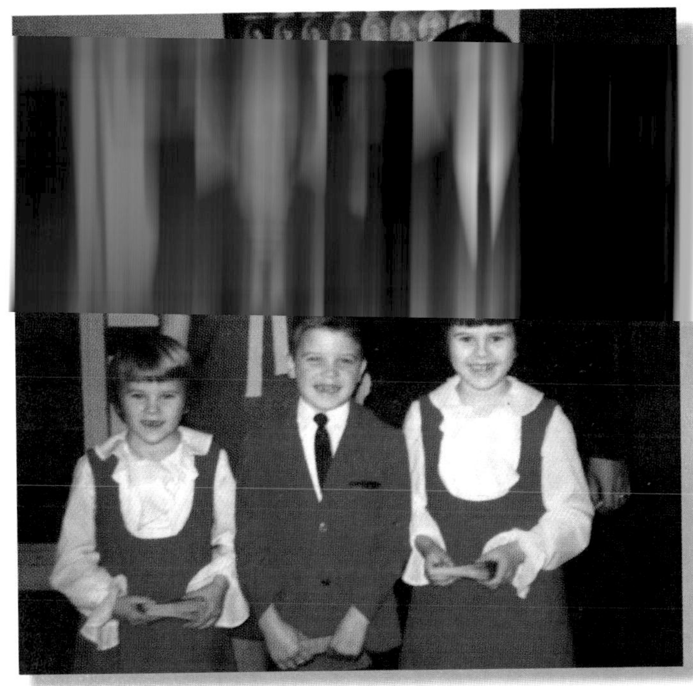

The Elways in the early 1960s.

Can you guess our family's favorite color?

Check out my snowball, ready for launch.

A bowling ball became an early favorite. We'd make a bowling alley in our hallway with plastic pins and balls.

I quickly learned a heavier ball knocked down more pins—and put more dents in the walls.

Soon, I graduated from rolling to throwing. Sports balls, dirt clods, rocks, snowballs—you name it, I threw them.

I mostly aimed at telephone poles and street signs but sometimes strayed and hit a window or two, angering neighbors and embarrassing Mom.

She always told me to be more careful, but Mom never told me to stop throwing balls.

Throwing a Wiffle ball in a neighbor's driveway almost cost me my young life.

I remember a group of us boys, all about ten years old, wanted to play baseball in a neighbor's driveway, but the neighbor's dog was sleeping in the middle of our "diamond."

We decided to play around the mutt. Everything was fine until I accidently stepped on the dog while pitching. Startled, the dog attacked me, leaping at my face and knocking me down. A neighbor rescued me and carried me home, my face and neck wrapped in a bloody towel. I needed five stitches on my chin and three on my neck, inches from my jugular vein.

My other close call came years later when I panicked on a bike and tumbled into a ditch. The hot red high-bar Stingray bike was my first with handbrakes.

My parents explained how to use the brakes, and I said, "I know, I know, I know."

The first trip down the street I went as fast as I could. As I neared the end of the street, I rotated the foot pedals backward, forgetting about the handbrakes. I crashed into the ditch. Luckily, I escaped with just cuts and bruises.

For a while, it seemed I had to learn all my lessons the hard way.

John was difficult to play against in board games. He wanted you to play your hardest.

My parents taught us about competing as far back as I can remember. We'd make simple things a competition.

One of our favorites came at nighttime. Mom and Dad used to time how fast we could put on our pajamas and get in bed. We fell for the trick every time. We loved earning the satisfaction of setting a new world record each night.

My sisters and I competed fiercely. I shared a room with Jana then and slept on top of the bunk bed. One night the girls hid the bed ladder so I would lose the race into bed.

In school, we'd compete to see who could get the best grades (I earned A's and B's and never got a C until I went to college). My parents cared more about effort than grades, though.

Whenever we swam, we'd stage diving competitions with Dad as judge.

The most intense family battles, however, involved board games.

We'd play Risk for days. We'd load up armies against each other and attack, both on and off the board. We'd fight about who cheated and who had picked on whom.

Finally my parents had to outlaw the game in our house for family sanity.

We played cards and other games, including Battleship and Monopoly. But many nights the games ended in fits and flopped boards.

My competitive spirit surfaced in school, too, with negative results.

We uprooted during the middle of my kindergarten school year in Aberdeen and moved to Missoula, Montana.

Jana and I didn't go back to school until that next fall. I didn't handle the change and new school too well. I spent many hours in the principal's office for being disruptive in class from the first grade through third.

Then my strict third-grade teacher found a solution. I somehow thought being the first to finish school work was more important than getting the right answers. I'd race through my work and then goof off.

Ms. Haynes met with my parents and devised a plan to settle me down. Since I loved sports, I took the newspaper's sports section to school every day. When I finished my work, I'd read about sports, and that kept me out of trouble (most of the time).

Even today, my kids call me "Newspaper Nose" because I can spend hours reading a newspaper.

It was snowing, and Christmas trees were being delivered to a school parking lot to be sold. Some friends and I tried hookey bobbing (grabbing the back bumper of a car with feet skidding on the snow) during recess. A teacher caught us and gave us three or four whacks each to remind us about the dangers of hookey bobbing. Now, in many states it is illegal for teachers to spank children.

I'd follow my favorite teams through the newspapers and whenever they were on television.

I liked the Dallas Cowboys with quarterback Roger Staubach and running back Calvin Hill. The Lakers and

me the day-to-day support I needed. She put in what I call "windshield time." She drove me to all my practices and games as I grew (one of the first things I bought after joining the NFL was a new car for Mom).

She even helped me learn how to throw. During my early elementary days, we'd play catch all the time after school, especially with a baseball. I'd pitch to her, and then she'd pitch to me. Soon, I started throwing too hard for her. Dad stopped catching my fastballs when I was 12 because they bruised his hand.

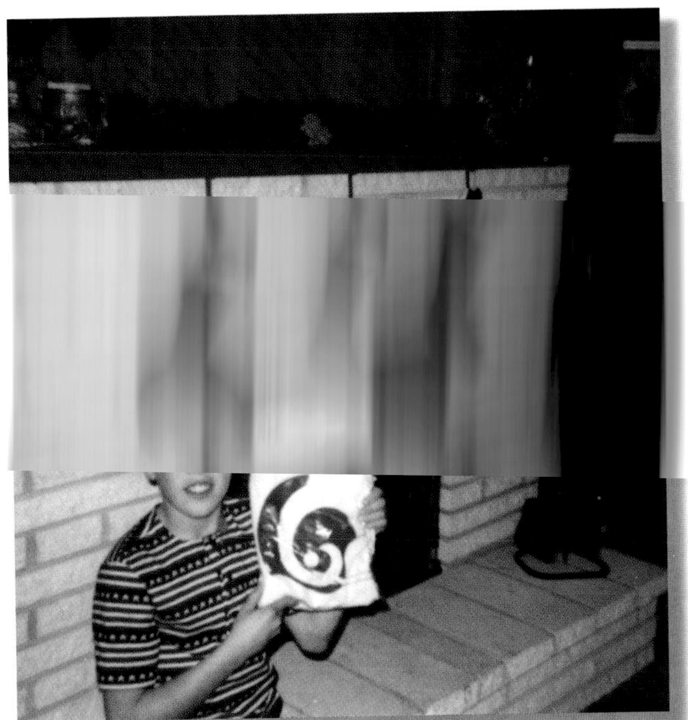

Receiving any type of sports gear made me smile.

Jack Elway

"I never pushed John to play sports. He was always there waiting for me on the steps when I got home. I wanted him to have fun and be as good as he could be. I think the greatest learning takes place in a positive atmosphere. Now, if he acted like a little jerk, he found that didn't pay off. I saw to it he didn't win our one-on-one games. It was a positive atmosphere with discipline within it."
—Jack Elway, John's father

Whenever Dad was home, we spent time together playing sports one-on-one. Dad built a basketball hoop every place we lived. We played against each other all the time. Dad would pretend to be a radio announcer, calling out the action as it happened. Sometimes Dad would let me win, and other times he'd play me tough.

We'd also go to a nearby field and throw the football or baseball. Dad carried a sack of equipment in his car for all three sports.

The family's competitive spirit increased when my parents bought a Ping-Pong table. We played for hours, but it always came down to Dad and I going head-to-head late into the night. Our downstairs must have smelled like a gym, as Dad and I would peel off our sweat-drenched shirts midway through our marathon games. Mom had to break us up so we'd finally go to bed.

I seemed to have a knack for picking up sports easily. One reason was I listened to Dad's instructions. Since he was a coach, I respected what he said about sports and techniques, so my ears were a sponge to his words.

Dad would show me correct sports techniques. The best part was he would keep it simple and explain why one way was better

[illegible]

to a nearby frozen pond in Montana. Without knowing what to do, Lee Ann, Jana, and I rushed onto the ice to see who could master the family's new sport first.

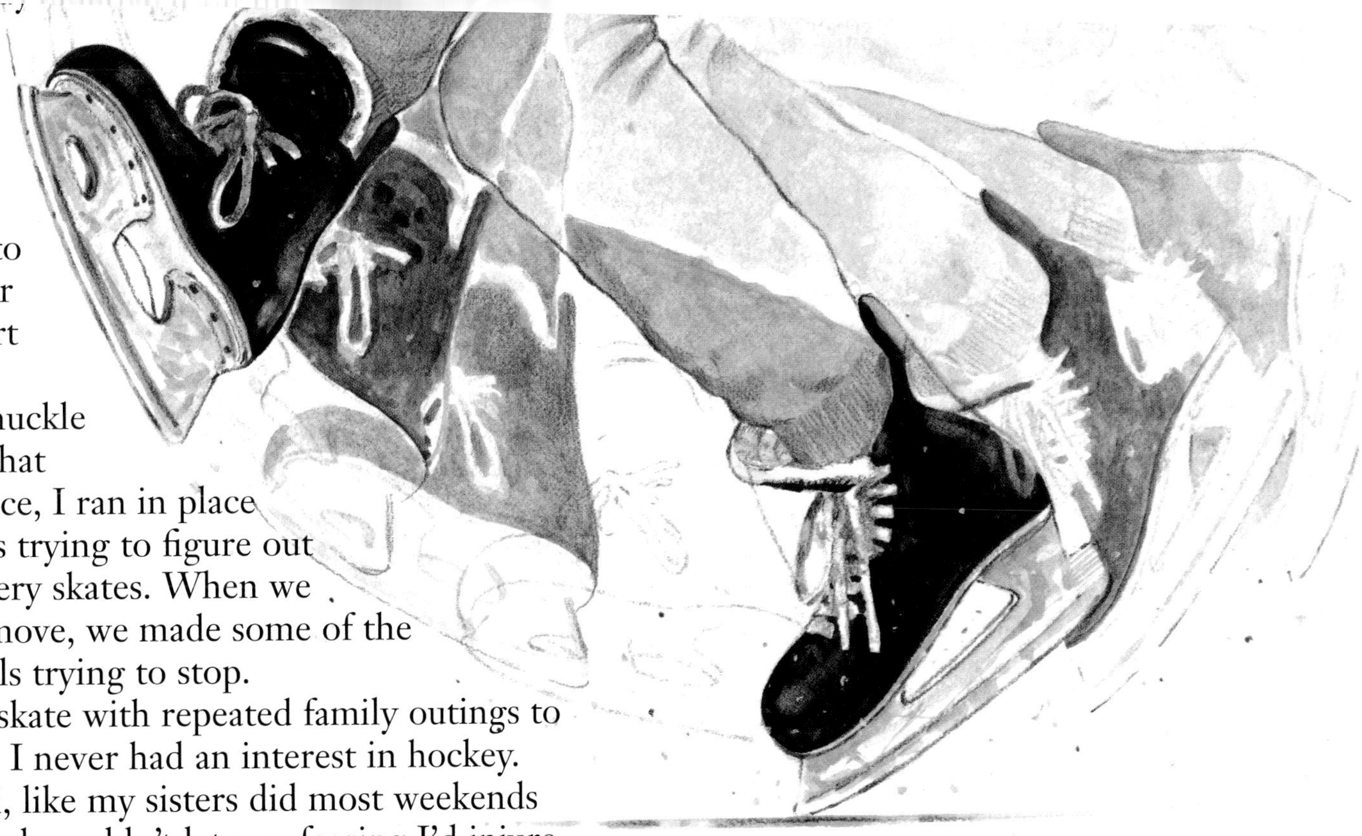

My parents still chuckle just thinking about that scene. Once on the ice, I ran in place for about 20 minutes trying to figure out how to use the slippery skates. When we figured out how to move, we made some of the greatest all-time spills trying to stop.

We all learned to skate with repeated family outings to the ice pond. Oddly, I never had an interest in hockey. I wanted to snow ski, like my sisters did most weekends in the winter, but Dad wouldn't let me, fearing I'd injure a knee.

I was late to John's first football game. I walked in at halftime and remember seeing a basketball coach I knew walking out. "Either those players are the worst I've ever seen or your son is the best player I've ever seen," the coach said.
—Jack Elway

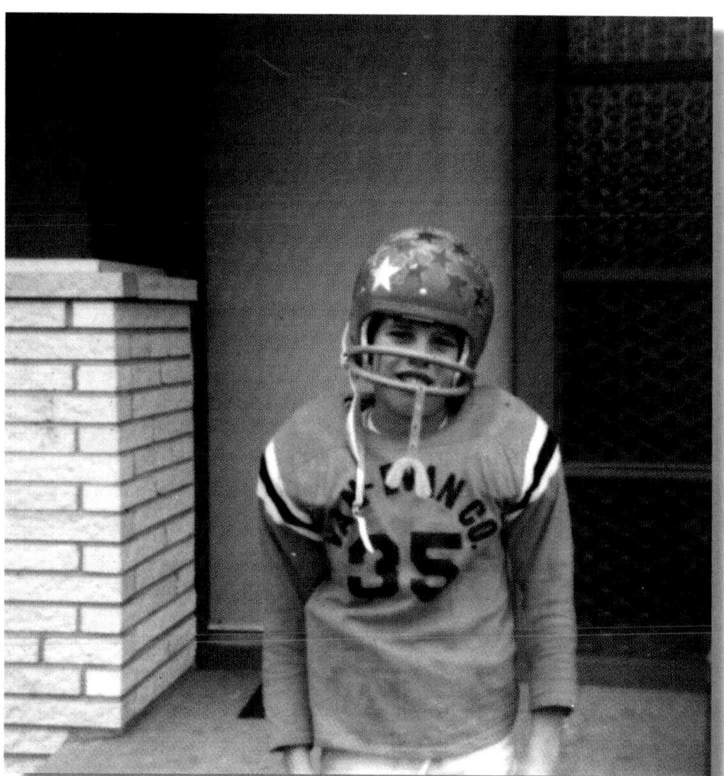
I dreamed of being Cowboy running back Calvin Hill (who also wore number 35). (Calvin Hill is father of NBA star Grant Hill.)

I wanted to play organized football as soon possible. So the summer I turned eleven, I signed up to play Little Grizzly football.

I remember Dad couldn't be there for signup. He said: "Now, John, when they ask you what position you want to play, you tell them you're a quarterback."

But I didn't want to play quarterback because I thought it would be boring just handing off the football. So I asked to be a running back but didn't tell Dad about it.

Dad arrived at halftime for my first game because of his football job. By then I had already run for four touchdowns. He was on time for my next game, and I scored on runs the first two times I touched the ball.

Dad never mentioned playing quarterback that season—that talk would come later. As the fastest runner in the league, I scored many touchdowns that season. Coaches awarded helmet stars for making big plays, and I wore mine proudly.

My first football season ended with a dramatic finish.

Our team, Evans Vance Co., won our city championship by beating Stockman's in overtime.

After tasting the sweetness of winning a championship, I knew I wanted more. I also knew I never wanted to play quarterback because being a running back was so much fun.

By the time I started playing Little League baseball at age ten people were already talking about me.

I'll be the first to say that at times I could be a brat on the field. Before every game, Mom would jokingly say, "Don't embarrass me!"

The top picture was taken in our backyard. The bottom picture shows me catching and Dad umpiring a game. During that game I caused a scene. First, I didn't like catching much and didn't always try my best. Our pitcher kept throwing balls in the dirt. Instead of blocking them, I'd wave my mitt at the bouncing balls.

One pitch got past me and smacked Dad's foot. He stopped the game and yelled at me in front of everyone: "Block the ball!" Dad corrected me whenever I threw a bat or helmet out of frustration.

The other time I upset Dad happened in the Montana Little League all-star state championship game. I was the only 11-year-old on the 12-year-old all-star team and didn't play much. I pouted and wouldn't talk to anyone and had tears in my eyes because I didn't play in the title game. Later, I got an earful from Dad about supporting the team even if I wasn't playing.

I learned about treating game officials with respect during a youth basketball game. Dad noticed me mouthing off and questioning their calls. During halftime, he took me behind the gym and told me to knock it off. Then he had the coaches bench me the rest of the game so I would remember the lesson.

It didn't take long for me to follow Dad's philosophy: Play hard all the time, be a team player, and respect coaches and officials.

I could be real stubborn at times, and my parents sometimes got in my face, including my grandmother (above). But I could also turn on the charm, as I did in this picture with Nannie before a family wedding.

I did have my lapses. One came on the practice field. Dad and I used to have batting practice by ourselves, which I always enjoyed. But one day, when I was about eleven years old, I invited a couple of friends.

Dad explained that a good host should let his friends hit first. I begrudgingly went to the outfield and just stood there, refusing to go after balls hit anywhere close to me.

After my friends batted, Dad told us to pick up the balls to go home, without allowing me a turn to hit.

At home, Dad spanked me for the first and only time of my life.

A babysitter once saved me from what might have been a worse punishment.

I used to pass time in Montana by throwing rocks, or hitting them with a bat, from our gravel road into the woods. One day I decided to hit rocks toward a neighbor's house. Before I knew it, I hit about 1,000 rocks into their yard.

The babysitter made me pick up every rock, which took four hours, and return them to our driveway before the neighbors—or my parents—came home.

Those tough early lessons showed me that changing a bad attitude is always possible.

In the fall of 1972, this is what my bedroom looked like.

Some of those trophies came from punt, pass, and kick competitions.

While I had a strong throwing arm, I didn't throw the football as well as you might think. Since I didn't want to play quarterback, I didn't work on the proper throwing motion until high school.

I reached the district level a couple of times before being eliminated. What crushed me the most was knowing that one more victory would have earned me a cool football uniform.

A few awards came from AAU track meets, where I won sprint races.

One day I was out painting the house, and John asked if he could have $5. I thought he wanted it to go to the store or something. Later, I found out he used it to enter a nearby AAU track meet. While painting, I heard a stadium announcer say: "100-yard winner, John Elway."
—Jack Elway

Unfortunately, my blazing foot speed stayed in Montana when Dad took a job as an assistant football coach at Washington State [illegible] to Pullman.

[illegible]

My spirits [illegible] one day in a sprint race. I suffered relentless teasing at school and at home.

I told Dad I wanted to quit track. But he made me stick out the season. "You started it, you finish it," he said. I tried other events, even pole vault and high jump, yet never found success on the track.

That fall Dad convinced me to try out for quarterback.

The move to Pullman was difficult in many ways.

I had a hard time sleeping in our new house because my room was too quiet. My room in Montana was next to our laundry room. Mom worked days as a secretary, so the washer and dryer were often running at night. The rhythmic tumbling always soothed me to sleep.

But in Pullman my room was away from the laundry.

Sometimes, after junior high school or on weekends, I'd nap on top of the running washer and dryer. Even today I can't sleep in silence, so we leave the bedroom TV on. And believe it or not, I still lay my head on the same pillow I've had since sixth grade.

Dad's job allowed me access to college facilities and athletes. I worked the sidelines each fall as the ballboy for Dad's college teams. And before school started, I'd go with Dad and live in the college dorms a few weeks during summer practices.

I loved being around the players. Even when a player at the University of Montana locked me in his closet a short time as a joke, I didn't mind. I felt special when players paid attention to me or let me play cards with them.

I had an up-close view of how hard they worked at practice and the highs and lows of sports. Seeing 275-pound linemen cry in the locker room after a tough loss showed me that competition at a high level always has its price.

The Cowboys' summer training camp was about 45 minutes from Granada Hills. Dad used his coaching connections to take me to the camp and watch. I met all the star players, including my heroes Staubach and Hill. Dad scouted for the Cowboys a few years and even wrote a fake scouting report on me. Dad wrote "bad attitude" because I wasn't doing my house chores at the time.

Dallas Cowboys Scouting Report

Player: John Elway
Age: 12
Strengths: Great arm, speed, outstanding student, knows the game.
Weakness: A bad attitude.

My eighth- and ninth-grade football seasons were unspectacular. Our offense did not pass much, and my enthusiasm for the sport slipped.

Moving from a small town to the largest urban area in the West proved a culture shock. Dad's rejection became an opportunity for me to test myself against some of the top high school athletes in the country.

We settled in Granada Hills, about 45 miles north of Los Angeles. The high school had a long tradition of winning, and coach Jack Neumeier loved the pass, sometimes calling for 40 a game.

I practiced hard on my throwing that summer, finally figuring out the difference between throwing a baseball and football. I learned to visualize throwing a football over a rope. This keeps my release point as high as possible, instead of throwing sidearm as some do with a baseball.

I started the season on the junior-varsity team as I learned the complicated passing system. Midway into the season, Neumeier made me the varsity starter. Many people questioned his wisdom.

At first, I felt intimidated by the size and speed of the varsity players. But after a few games I felt more confident. We finished my sophomore season 6-4 and made the playoffs.

Herb Carleton, Los Angeles Daily News

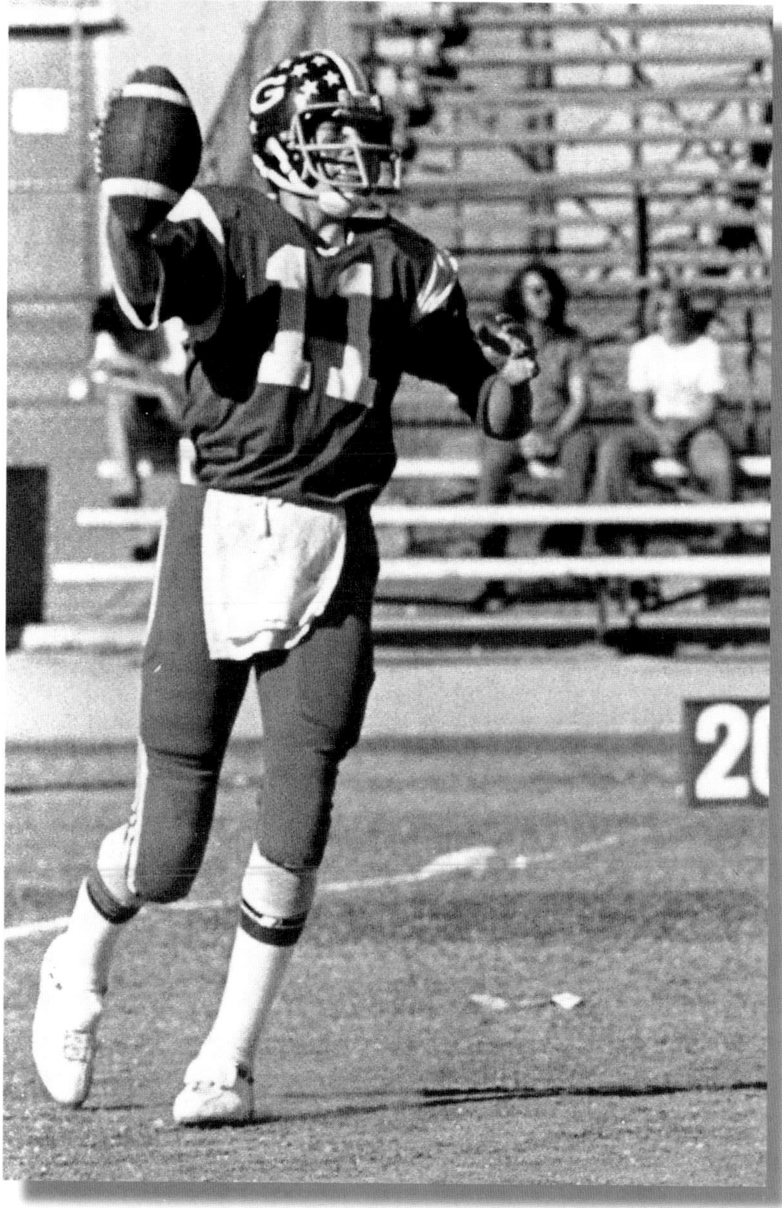

John completed 60 percent of his passes in high school for 5,711 yards and 49 touchdowns. He was named to All-America teams his junior and senior seasons.

I worked harder that summer to improve. That meant sometimes saying "no" to friends. While friends spent the summer at the beach, I spent much of my time practicing passing plays with receivers or playing in a summer passing league. To improve my accuracy, I'd hit the goal posts from 35 yards out or have someone throw a football into the air from 40 yards away and hit it in midair with a pass.

I did hang out with friends and go to the beach occasionally, although I never tried surfing. To be good at anything takes practice. And to practice enough means sometimes saying "no" to friends.

That extra effort started paying off my junior year. Our team made it to the semifinals of the city championships.

One of the most memorable games was against Fernando High—a game we won twice.

With 11 seconds left, I threw a 35-yard touchdown pass. But officials called a penalty on our team, nullifying the score. We huddled again with no time on the clock, and the coaches yelled in from the sidelines, "Same play!" I found the same receiver for another game-winning touchdown.

Going into my senior football season, coach Neumeier set a goal for me to pass for 5,000 yards. Expectations were high.

locker room. There, Dad asked me what I wanted to do—stay or go to the hospital. I responded: "Tape me up." Dad did, and I played the second half. Hobbling on one leg, I threw a touchdown, but we still lost.

My worst fears came true when doctors discovered my knee needed

for the basketball season. That spring I played baseball, and we won our second straight city championship, with the title game in Dodger Stadium.

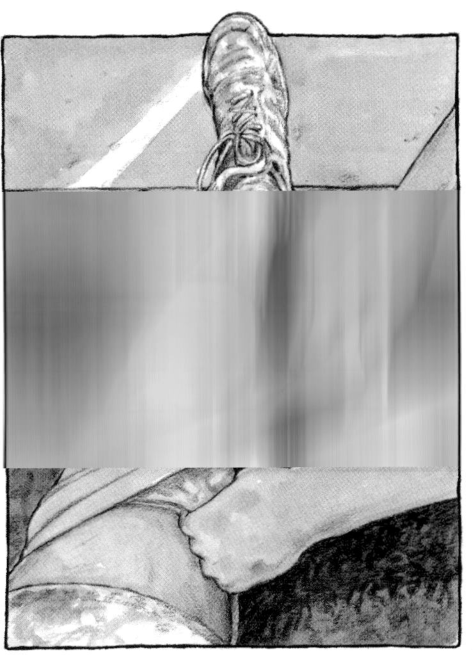

"John never acted like a big shot. He never asked for favors. He'd do everything everybody else would do. He was really kind of shy at first, just like any tenth-grader. His whole life was sports. He had all the things you'd want in a quarterback, and he didn't let success go to his head. He was a real good kid." —Granada Hills football coach Jack Neumeier.

Nuemeier

Herb Carleton, Los Angeles Daily News

"John wasn't very vocal. He led by doing. He once caught a line drive at third base with his barehand and turned a double play. In the city championship game, he saved us with terrific relief pitching. Just as important, he had an outstanding attitude. I never saw him have a bad day. He loved to play and loved to practice. And you could count on John. My 5-year-old son was the batboy , and he idolized John. He asked John to come to one of his T-ball games. John promised he would. On prom day, John showed up at my son's game—with his date—and watched for two hours." —Granada Hills baseball coach Daryl Stroh

Stroh

My knee problem helped me realize that nothing in sports is guaranteed. Dad told me how an injury cut short his college football career, and he always stressed the importance of getting a college degree. Whenever my parents talked about the future with us kids, they'd start a sentence saying: "After you graduate from college . . ." They put that expectation of going to college in our brains early on.

Another thing Dad always said was to let the future take care of itself and enjoy each season on its own.

I have always loved hanging out with teammates off the field. It's important to me to be one of the guys and make friendships.

Like everyone in high school, I struggled with peer pressure. Some friends wanted to do things I thought weren't right—like drinking beer and using illegal drugs. I managed to stay away from both, mostly because I didn't want to break the trust of my parents.

Mom and Dad never gave me a curfew. After our night games, I'd always go home for an hour to talk about the game. Then Dad would ask what time I'd be back. I picked a reasonable time, like midnight, and stuck to it.

I wasn't perfect. I did some stupid things in high school, like throw oranges and lemons at moving cars (thankfully we didn't cause an accident). Overall, however, I felt proud to make good decisions and stay out of trouble. It wasn't until I graduated and read things that people wrote in my annual that I realized how students can be role models to each other.

This picture is one of my sisters and me during high school. Jana (left) and Lee Ann are married with two children each.

This photo shows Jana and me on senior prom night. No, I didn't take Jana. This was taken at home before we met up with our dates.

Granada Hills High School

John, You know people don't know the real you. You have the kind of personality that not too many people have. You don't let things go to your head. -Don

Hey Superstar, What I would really like to say is that you have many other attributes other than your overriding physical ability, which I don't believe you know. Remember that with your physical talents you have many qualities of your mind. If you really develop both, John, your success will be great. -Tim

John, This is hard to say, but honestly you are the person I most look up to being able to achieve what I have always dreamed of, and you've always kept your class! Your friend, Steve

John, You're the humblest "stud" I know. I really appreicated you being such a nice guy to a mere junior as I was. Your friend always, Gene

John, You're a man to remember and admire. You're a great guy and great athlete. Good luck, Scott

Dear John, I'm glad I've gotton a chance to know you. I read about you in the papers everyday! I think you handle the publicity you get much better than anyone else ever could. I think as a person you have lots of great qualities. Love always, Kristi

Sports Illustrated, Richard Mackson

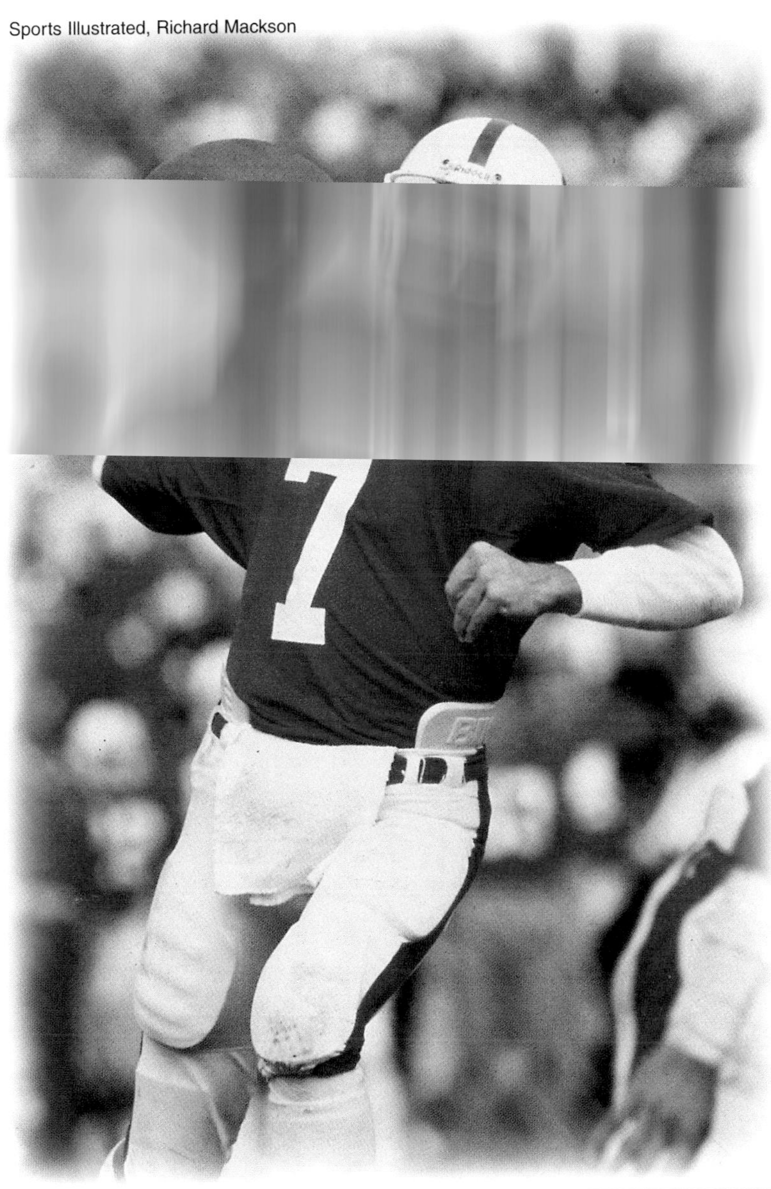

One of my dreams through high school was to play college football in the Pac-10 Conference.

About 65 colleges were after me. I decided

Jose State played in a league less competitive than the Pac-10. I struggled with the choice.

Finally, I told Dad, "If you really want me to go to San Jose State, I will."

Dad could have selfishly convinced me to play for his team, but he showed true parental love by doing what was best for me at his own expense. Dad gave me his blessing to attend Stanford.

I made an impact as a freshman, splitting playing time with returning senior Turk Schonert. Before my college career started, however, I fell flat on my face.

Running onto the field for my first college play, I caught my toe on the turf and tripped, landing face first. Talk about embarrassing!

Stanford coaches realized John had special talents right away, and so did Stanford receivers. John threw the football so hard, the tip of the football left a bruised impression on the chests and arms of those who tried to catch his passes. The bruises became known as the "Elway Cross."

One time in practice, a hard Elway pass broke a Cardinal receiver's finger so badly the jagged bone popped through his skin.

After a 2-0-1 start, we lost our final three Pac-10 games to finish 5-5-1. I became the starter my sophomore year and caught national attention by passing for 27 touchdowns and 2,889 yards, earning All-America honors. Unfortunately, all those yards and touchdowns equated to just a 6-5 season, my only winning year at Stanford.

An ankle injury hampered my junior year as we finished 4-7.

By the end of my senior year I had set five national passing records and nine Pac-10 marks. But still we were 5-6, and I never played in a bowl game for Stanford.

My four years at Stanford produced some great memories on and off the field. I experienced thrilling victories and crushing defeats.

A memorable play came against USC. I dropped back to pass and scrambled backward, drifting 30 yards behind the line of scrimmage. Then I found a receiver deep behind the Trojan defenders and launched a pass that went 72 yards in the air for a touchdown.

My final Stanford game proved the most painful. A victory against cross-bay rival California would have put us in a bowl game. But after a last-minute go-ahead drive for a field goal, Cal received the kickoff with just 4 seconds left. What followed will be remembered as one of the wildest, most controversial finishes ever. Cal players lateralled the ball wildly five times before being tackled and scored the winning touchdown by running over our band members, who stormed the field thinking we had won.

Sports Illustrated, Richard Mackson

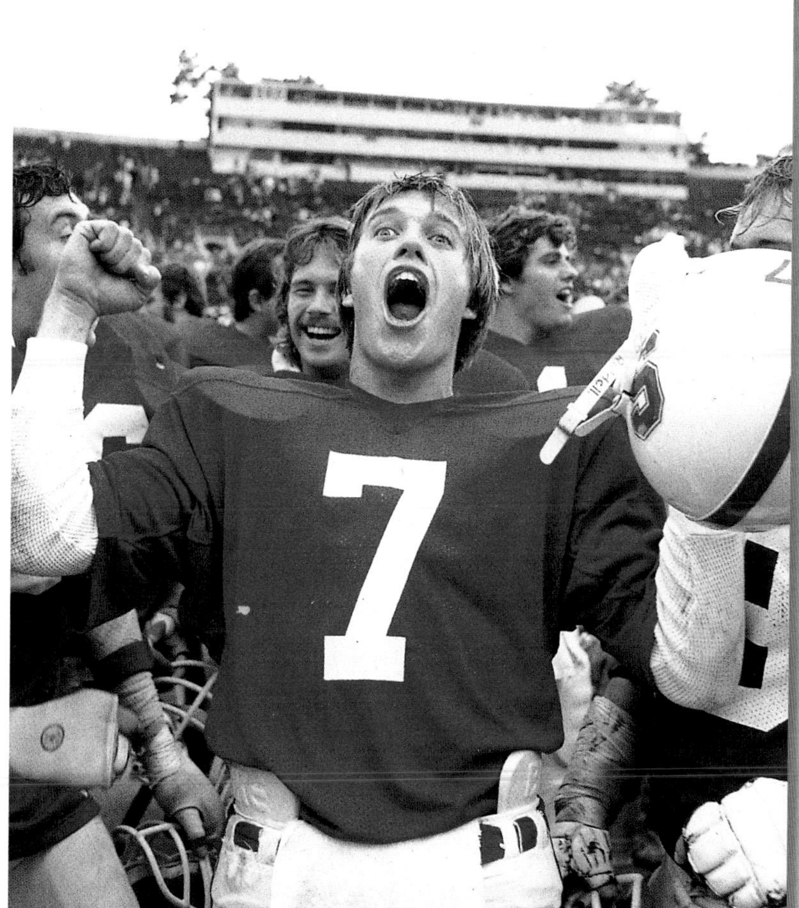

We had our share of upset victories, including this one over No. 1-ranked Washington.

I didn't achieve all my goals at Stanford, but I wouldn't trade that time in college for anything.

day. The West lost, but I was named the game's Most Valuable Player.

Ironically, the year after I left, Stanford hired Dad as their new head football coach.

Before graduating from Stanford, however, I received an education in the real world thanks to the National Football League's draft.

John and his father.

David Madison

I played baseball my first two years at Stanford. The first season, I hit only .269 with one home run. I considered quiting baseball. But Cardinal coach Mark Marquess convinced me to stick with it. During a few weeks in the spring, I had football and baseball on the same day.

My second college baseball season showed vast improvement. I batted .361 and belted nine home runs. I can thank an old high school buddy for one homer. He played for Arizona State as a catcher. We were way ahead when I stepped to the plate. He whispered: "Here comes a fastball." I belted one of my longest home runs. Another game, I made all three outs in an inning from right field by throwing runners out.

An NCAA rule allowed me to play professional baseball the summer of my junior year and still keep my college football status. The New York Yankees signed me to play six weeks in Oneonta, New York, in the Class A league. I started off 1 for 19 at the plate, but finished hitting .318 with a team-leading 25 runs batted in.

The Colts, then in Baltimore, owned the first pick in the 1983 NFL draft because they were winless the previous season.

Thanks to that summer of baseball with the Yankees, I had a choice to play either pro football or baseball. Before the draft, I warned the Colts not to draft me. I wanted to play for a West Coast team to be close to family and friends, and I had no interest in playing for the Colts' owner or coach at the time.

On draft day I watched TV in shock as the Colts drafted me anyway. What was supposed to be one of the happiest days in my life turned ugly.

A standoff lasted for weeks as I considered playing professional baseball.

Finally, the Colts traded me to Denver, which delighted me.

Many people called me spoiled for forcing the Colts' hand. Looking back, I know I did the right thing. I worked hard in both sports to be in a position to say no to the Colts. Plus, I was honest with the Colts about my intentions.

The only thing I regret is not communicating well enough that my problem was with the Colts' management, not the city.

The Broncos signed me to a five-year, $5 million deal, making me the highest paid NFL player before my first game. The pressure to perform rested squarely on my shoulders.

I won the starting job in training camp, but I really wasn't ready to be an NFL starter.

Sports Illustrated, Carl Iwasaki

AP/Wide World Photos

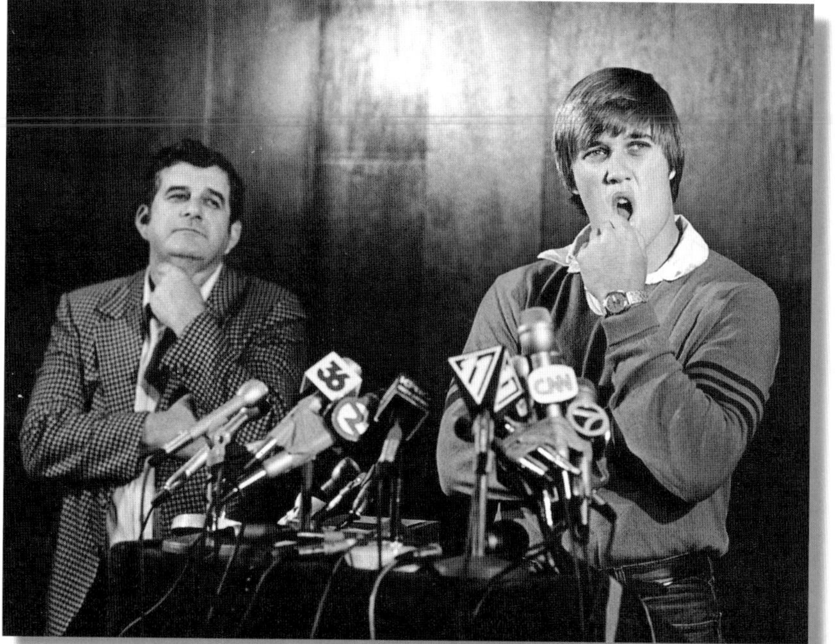

I figuratively fell flat on my face that first season in Denver.

My first game, against Pittsburgh, I connected on just one of eight passes and needed help from veteran QB Steve DeBerg for the win.

The next game was in Baltimore, and Colts fans let me have it. I had death threats before the game. People threw glass bottles at me and cursed me during the game. That's the only time I've kept my chin strap on the entire game.

Again DeBerg relieved me for a win.

The next three games were disasters. One game I became so mixed up I lined up for the center snap behind our guard. Everyone in the stands laughed at me. TV commentators asked: "Is Elway a $5 million mistake?"

For the first time in my sports career I was benched (in the sixth week). Never before had I felt such criticism. Self-doubt crawled into my head, and I wondered if I could make it in the NFL.

One rookie game worth remembering was our rematch against Baltimore at Denver. I earned my first come-from-behind victory with three TD passes in the fourth quarter.

I talked out my rookie frustrations with people close to me. Dad always has been a great listener and my real backbone. Through those tough times Dad and I became more than father and son—we became friends.

Mom, my sisters, and college friends pumped me back up, too. My girlfriend from college, Janet, lived in Seattle that season. I called her about twenty-four times a week. She became my emotional cheerleader thanks to her positive outlook.

Nobody can make it alone. And I couldn't have made it through the year without her and my support team.

Janet and I formed our own team three months after my first season ended. We invited 800 of our closest friends to our wedding.

Luckily, we both overlooked first impressions. I remember the first time I saw Janet, at a Stanford swim meet. When she got out of the water, I thought she looked like a wet rat. Janet remembers looking up at me during the meet and "seeing some guy with a goofy smile."

Janet first heard my name at a Stanford football game our freshman year. The crowd started chanting "El-way. El-way." Janet turned to a friend and asked: "What's an Elway?"

On our first date, when I tried to kiss her good night, we clanked front teeth. A few dates later I accidentally broke her pinky finger. We were playing toss with a football and she said: "Bring on the heat." So I did. We haven't played catch since.

It didn't take long for us to catch each other's hearts.

We dated one month before I knew she was the love of my life. Before we graduated from Stanford, I asked her out on what I called "our last date." I took her to Coit Tower in San Francisco, a 210-foot romantic building overlooking the Bay Area. I got down on one knee and asked her to marry me. We celebrated our 10th anniversary with a trip back to Coit Tower.

Janet, who started swimming at age 5, had an outstanding college career. She led Stanford to a national title in 1980 as the team's top meet scorer with 82 points in five events. She set a national record in the 400 I.M. and was in position to make the Olympic team. But the U.S. boycotted the 1980 Games in Moscow. Politics sadly crushed the life-long Olympic dreams of Janet and many other U.S. athletes.

After our honeymoon, I felt renewed with the competitive fire to improve.

I worked out five days a week in

My confidence grew with each victory as we set a regular-season team record with a 13-3 mark before a first-round playoff loss to Pittsburgh ended the season.

During my third year I set five Denver offensive records, but we failed to make the playoffs at 11-5.

The 1986 season proved to be a giant step forward with a trip to Super Bowl XXI. To get there, however, we needed a victory at Cleveland in the AFC championship game.

Freezing wind iced our faces as we huddled with 5½ minutes to play at our own 2-yard line. We needed a 98-yard touchdown drive to tie. Considering our last two drives went for only 9 and 6 yards, the task seemed impossible. Guard Keith Bishop broke the huddle tension by saying: “Now we’ve got them where we want them.”

AP/Wide World Photos

What followed became known as “The Drive.” As we marched down the field, everyone kept their cool and did their jobs. I hit 5 of 8 passes for 78 yards and ran for 20 more. We forced overtime with a 5-yard TD pass with 39 seconds left. Our defense held, and then we drove 60 yards to set up a game-winning field goal.

Performing under pressure—when the game is at stake—is what athletes dream of doing.

Since then I’ve been involved in other memorable drives—a 75-yard heart-stopper the next year to beat Cleveland again in the AFC title game, and a 98-yard, 107-second drive with no timeouts and two fourth-down plays against Houston in 1992.

Those tense endings are tougher on my wife than me.

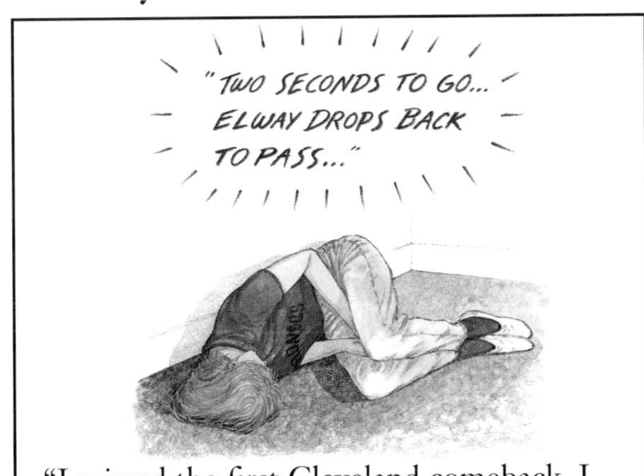

"TWO SECONDS TO GO...
ELWAY DROPS BACK
TO PASS..."

“I missed the first Cleveland comeback. I turned off the TV and decided to get out the Christmas stuff because I figured the season was over. The second Cleveland comeback, I wouldn’t watch. Instead, I laid on the stadium suite floor, and a friend gave play-by-play. Now, whenever we stage a comeback at Mile High Stadium, friends say: ‘Ok, Janet, go lie down in the corner.’ And I do.”—Janet Elway

AP/Wide World Photos

AP/Wide World Photos

Losing in the Super Bowl is gut-wrenching on everyone involved with the team—players, coaches, staff, management, and fans.

You work so hard to get to that point, and you are one win away from the ultimate of what you play for. There's not a worse loss. You're so close and expectations are so high, then you fall off the face of the earth.

The fact that we led at halftime in the first two Super Bowls only made the pain deeper. My only consolation has been that I've walked off three Super Bowl fields knowing I tried and did everything I possibly could to win.

JOHN'S SUPER BOWL STATS

Super Bowl XXI

N.Y. Giants 39, Denver 20

John passed for 304 yards, completing 22 of 37 passes for 1 TD. He ran for 1 score.

Super Bowl XXII

Washington 42, Denver 10

John passed for 257 yards on 14 of 38 passes for 1 TD, a 56-yarder that set a record for fastest score (1:57 into the game). Three passes were picked off.

Super Bowl XXIV

San Francisco 55, Denver 10

John passed for 109 yards with two interceptions, completing 10 of 26 attempts.

I was amazed how well John handled the Super Bowl losses. I could tell he was really sad. I know he really wanted to win. We all went to dinner after one of them, and John comforted everyone else. He took the attitude that there are worse things in life that could happen.
—Jana Elway

Marc Serota/EGI

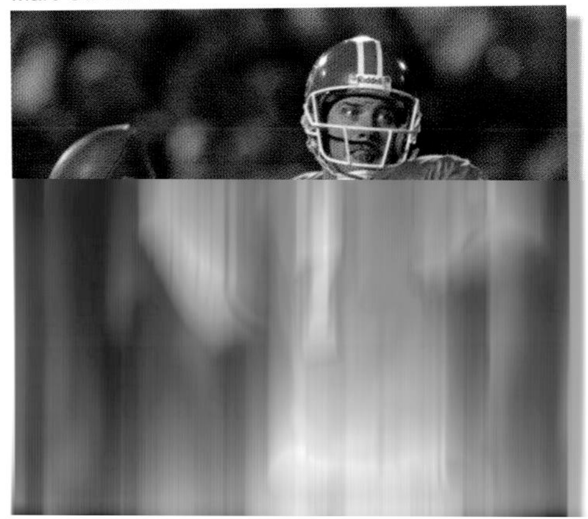

Allsport USA

And I mean trying everything. In the second Super Bowl, against Washington, I caught a pass—a first for a Super Bowl quarterback. We call the trick play a "throw-back." I hand the ball off and curl up field. The running back goes the opposite way, stops, and throws back to me. Ours went for 23 yards against Washington. I've caught four throwback passes so far in my career, but I'm happier throwing the ball.

Passing the football is what has kept me in the NFL. In 14 seasons my passes have traveled more than 45,000 yards (about 25 miles). Going into the 1997 season, only two other NFL quarterbacks have thrown for more yards—Dan Marino and Fran Tarkenton.

My ability to run away from would-be tacklers, known as scrambling, has been just as important as my right arm. It's hard to explain, but I can feel rushers. I can hear them coming, and sometimes their shadows give them away.

When I avoid rushers, that gives my receivers extra time to get open or provides a lane for me to pick up yards running.

My 3,000-plus rushing yards rank behind only Tarkenton when combined with passing (unfortunately I've been sacked for about 350 more yards than my rushes).

I'm honored my positive statistics place me in great company. But players who worry about stats and money don't perform as well as they could in a team sport. The bottom line, and my ultimate goal, always has been to win a Super Bowl.

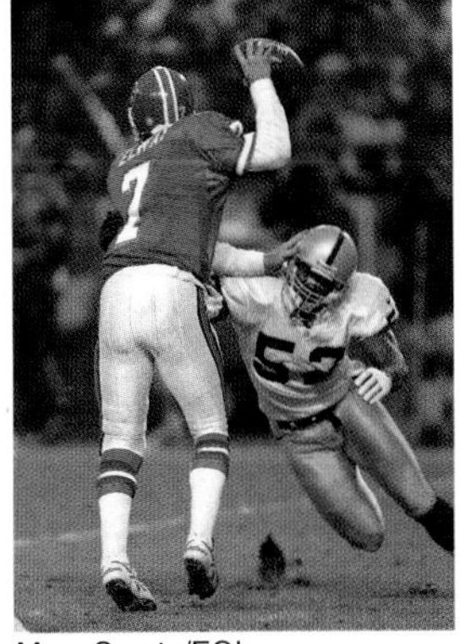

Marc Serota/EGI

Sports Illustrated, Walter Iooss, Jr.

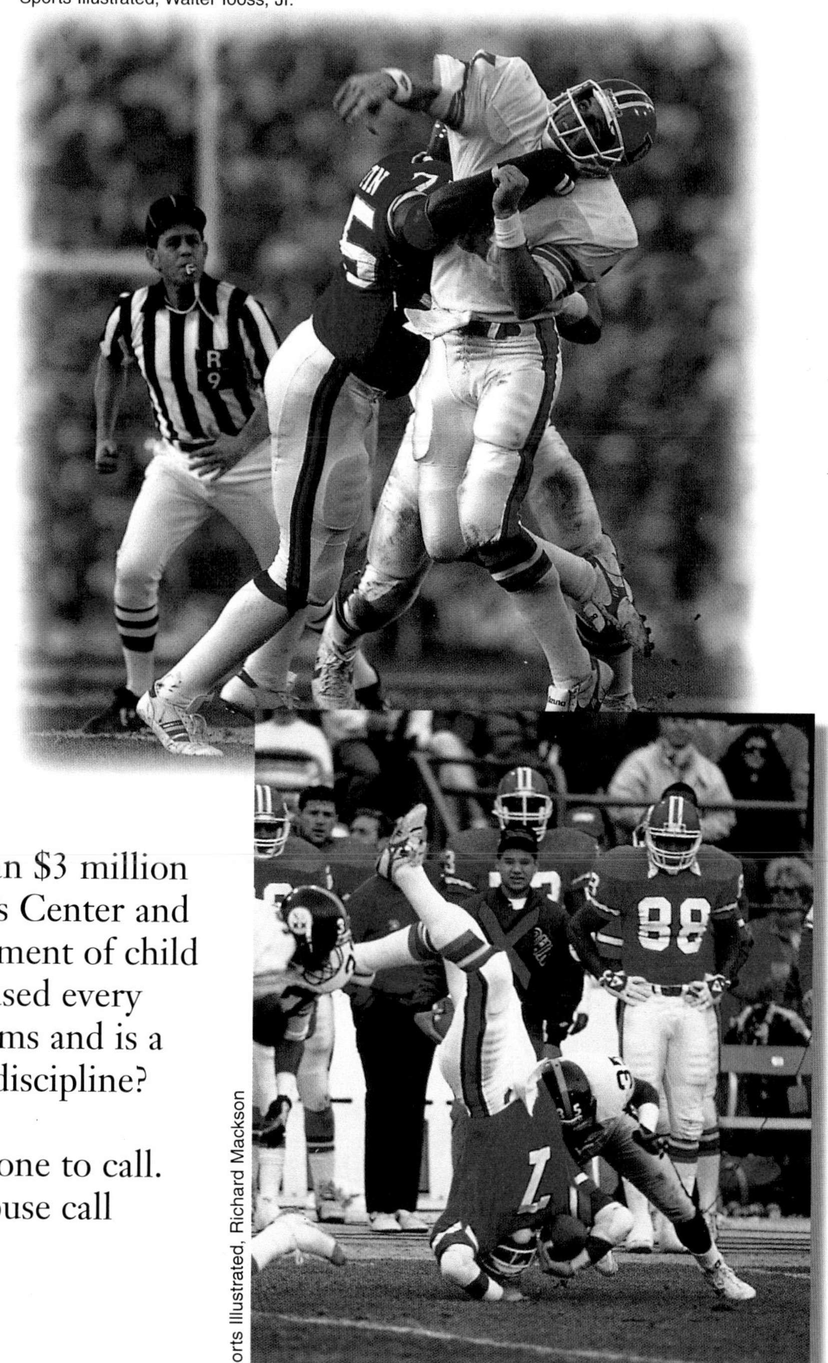

Sports Illustrated, Richard Mackson

Whatever success I've had on the field has extracted a price of pain. Dad always said if you expect something for nothing then the price is too high.

Hits are going to hurt when you play a contact sports like football. I've had five knee operations, a fractured rib, torn rotator cuff, groin and hamstring pulls, sprained elbows and fingers, countless bruises and turf burns, and one season a sore elbow that stung every time I threw. Still, in 14 seasons I missed just 15 games.

The fame of playing in the NFL has brought thousands of letters and requests from people, many of whom are in pain. Some want my autograph, others ask for help. Even if I didn't play football, there wouldn't be enough hours in a day to help everyone.

So I created a foundation that has raised more than $3 million for two Denver organizations: the Kempe Children's Center and F.A.C.E.S. Both focus on the preventation and treatment of child abuse. Did you know that 3 million children are abused every year in the United States? Abuse comes in many forms and is a complicated issue. When does spanking go beyond discipline? That's a tough call.

That's why Child Help USA has a hotline for anyone to call. If you, or someone you know, needs to talk about abuse call 1-800-4-A-CHILD (422-4453).

Marc Serota/EGI

The charity work I've done has opened my eyes to

or two when I tell my wife: "This is my last year."

Having the unconditional love of family, perspective, and a sense of humor is what helps me get through the pressure and frustration.

performance.

Janet and I have three daughters and a son. They all love me no matter what happens on the field.

NFL Photos, Rob Brown

"John, in parts . . ."

"Hey, this needs a tire . . ."

"I'll be back."

During my early years in Denver, I felt the world staring at me. The local media reported my every move—when I had haircuts, what I ate, what candy I gave out at Halloween. Someone probably counted the number of breaths I took in a day.

Whatever pressures I feel from football, my family helps me remember the important things in life.

Starting a car dealership business helped me balance sports with the real world. And when we aired silly television ads showing my goofy side, people saw me as a real person.

The light-hearted ads I've done for my business and the NFL have helped me laugh at myself. There were many times I thought I'd lose my sense of humor.

If you don't have a sense of humor, life can drive you right into the ground.

Glenn Asakawa, Rocky Mountain News

Marc Serota/EGI

As the seasons have passed, each year brings new challenges. People talk about my age and wonder if I still have what it takes to win in the NFL. After hearing so many negative questions about getting older, there were times when I felt older and slower. But you can't let negativity tackle you.

I've found age is more a mindset than a number. I decided to play and work out the only way I know how—all out with total commitment.

I work out about two hours a day, four days a week during the offseason. I find each year I have to work harder than the year before to stay in top physical shape.

regular-season record.

Many believed 1996 would finally be the year we brought home a Bronco Super Bowl trophy.

Our season ended with a stunning 30-27 home loss to the Jacksonville Jaguars in our first playoff game. We ran into a team that was playing as well as anyone that day, plus we didn't play our best game. The loss felt like a punch to the gut that knocks the wind out of you.

Losing always hurts me. If it didn't, that would mean I didn't care. In a strange way, losing has to hurt to make winning feel so good. But if you learn from defeat, then you don't have to accept losing as a loss.

AP/Wide World Photos

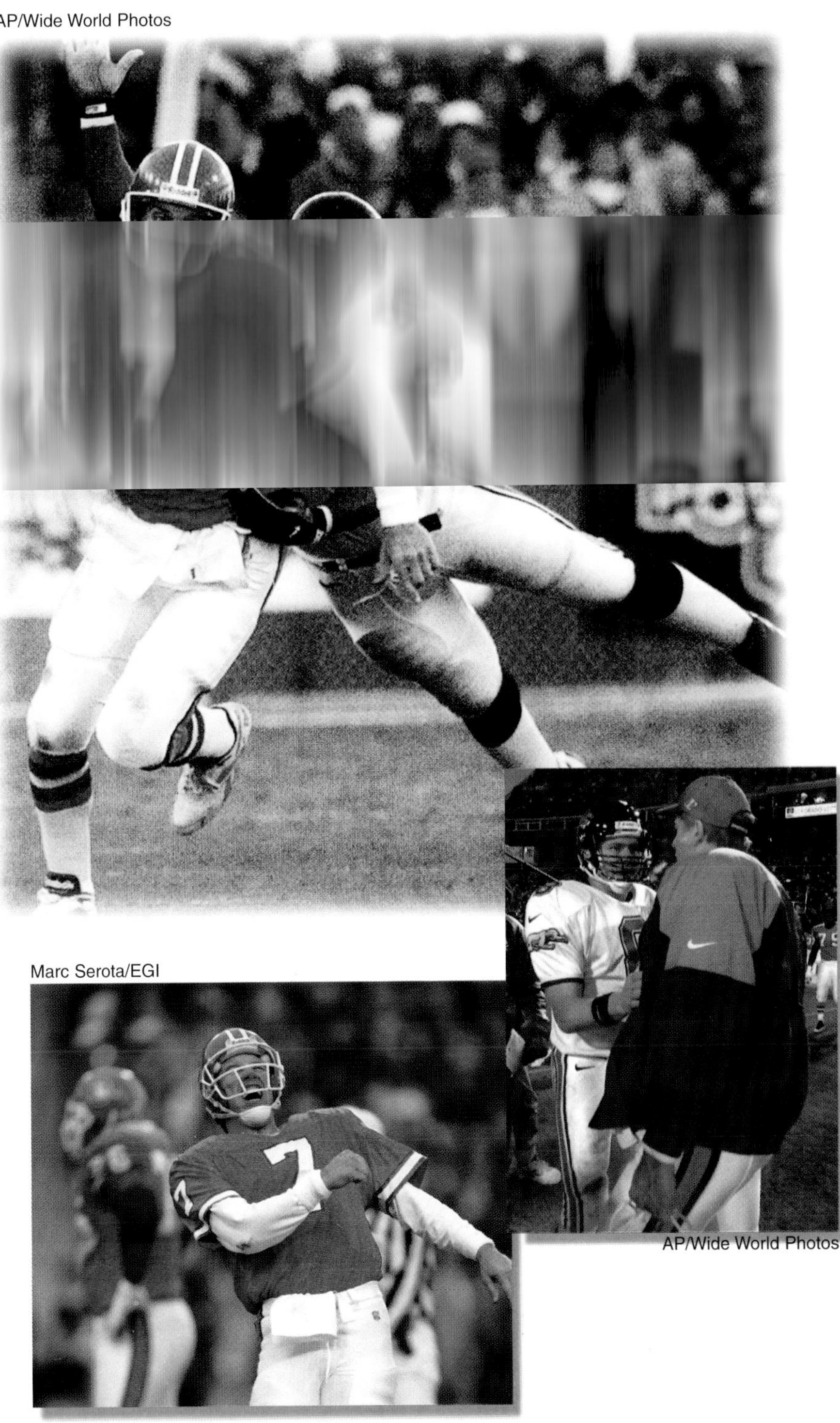

Marc Serota/EGI

AP/Wide World Photos

David Madison

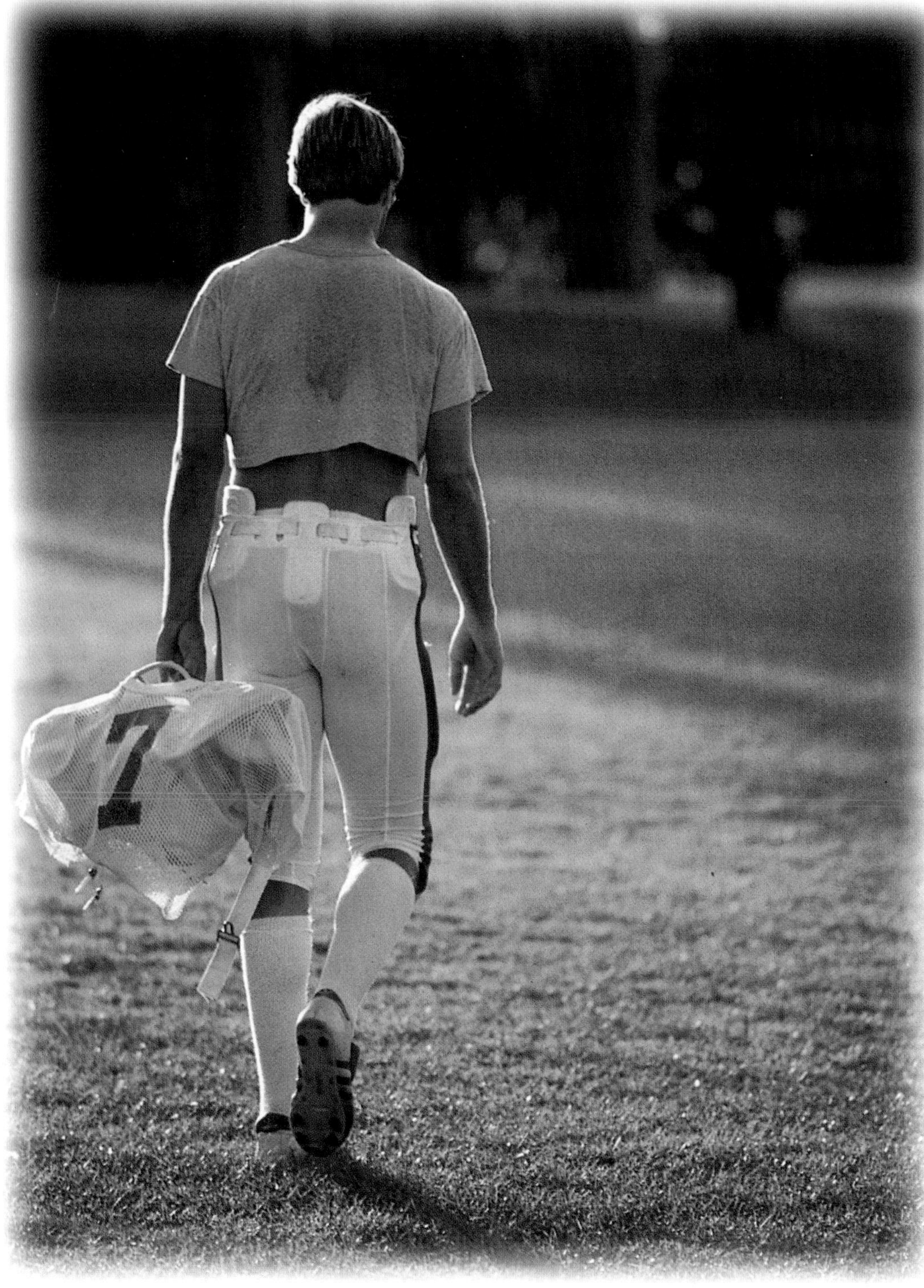

The thing I've noticed about people who are winners is that, to them, losing is always temporary. The great thing about playing sports—and about life—is you can always redeem yourself in the next game or the next season. A winner is someone who is able to come back from defeat.

Nobody knows how many next seasons any of us has. Even though I know my number is shrinking, every year I hold onto the dream of winning it all.

Until that last second has ticked in my last game, I will always try for one more comeback.

A favorite saying of Dad's is: When you've taken your last step, take one more.

That's sound advice for anyone who wants to be a comeback kid.